1

Ace of Diamonds Magic Company

presents

So you Want To Be

A Ventriloquist!

A Beginners Guide to Ventriloquism

By

Colin Dymond

First Published in 2014

ISBN #: 978-1-291-98490-3

Also by Colin Dymond

Making Magical Memories, A great guide for children's entertainers. Available direct from Colin.

The Magic of Puppets, a two disc DVD on how to incorporate magic routines with your puppets. Available direct from Colin or Practical Magic

Steve Axtell's Forward

Colin Dymond is not only one of the hardest working ventriloquists in the UK, he's also a good teacher of this magical skill!

He has been a Power User of Axtell Expressions puppets for many years and we have watched his shows get stronger and stronger.

Look for anything this performer touches to turn out fantastic and get your hands on any videos, books or teaching materials he releases.

He really understands the ins and outs and subtlies of puppets, manipulation and ventriloquism.

You will enjoy this!

Steve Axtell

Steve Axtell with the Magic Drawing Board with sticking out tongue!

Acknowledgements

It's been a long hard but fun road getting to where I am today and there are many that I need to thank.

Ray Alan, Shari Lewis and especially Jim Henson for showing what was possible with a puppet, I know Jim kept himself under the desk but what incredible creatures did he bring to life, and, he must have been the biggest employer of puppeteers ever!

Len Belmont for showing me the tricks of the trade.

Darryl Worbey for his brilliant workmanship on Snot the Dragon.

Steve Axtell for letting me spend so much money on his wonderful creations.

It can be a lonely life being a ventriloquist, there are not too many of us and we don't get to meet often but thanks to David Tomkins and Kieran Powell for sharing the madness.

Zoobee and Alec Powel for deciding that a UK ventriloquist convention was a good idea.

Richard Olpin for my great web site and brilliant photos' but I'm keeping my kit on!

To the Lovely Wendi, thanks for everything, way to much to list here but when I win the lottery you'll get paid. Love you!

And to my Brilliant Boys, I'm so proud of you both.

Preface

So you want to be a ventriloquist!

Why would someone write a book with such a title? Well, it's all the fault of a man called Zoobee or Shane West to give him his proper tittle, he came up with the idea of holding a convention in the UK for ventriloquists! He kindly asked if I could do a lecture teaching the basics of ventriloquism, the clever stuff he was going to leave to Mark Wade!

I jumped at the chance to be a part of the UKs first Ventarama and thought about what I could talk about. What did I think were the building blocks for being a good ventriloquist that would enable someone to put a show together.

There are two thoughts on lecture notes, one is that they should be just that, notes that help someone remember what they saw at the lecture; the other being, that a set of notes should be able to be read by someone who was not at the lecture and they should be able to gain all the knowledge that was emparted on that day maybe with some extras.

So what started as a set of notes for a one day convention, has ended up as what I hope is a full guide for anyone thinking of starting in ventriloquism which might also have some tips for those already some way down the path.

Enjoy the journey, it's meant to be fun.

Colin Dymond

2014

Contents

So You Want To Be A Ventriloquist

Why?

No seriously, why?

Fame?

If so then go ahead and name 10 living ventriloquists that are making real big bucks that the general public have heard of. At the time of writing this, in the UK we have Nina Conti who is on TV more than once a year, and then Paul Zerdin and Steve Hewlett who the public might have heard of.

DanPayes' Old Man in "Head to Head"

In the USA there is Terry Fator with his own theatre in Las Vegas and topping them all Jeff Dunham who is one of the biggest selling comedians in the world. That sounds great but that's five names and only two of them are earning big bucks.

Fortune?

Re read the last paragraph!

Although you might never make a fortune there are a lot of ventriloquists who make a reasonable living from talking to themselves either as pure ventriloquists or by using ventriloquism as part of a magic show.

Making you attractive to the opposite/same sex?

Now you are just being silly, can we get on with the actual book now please?

Good Reasons for Being a Ventriloquist.

Ventriloquism is in essence a double act, most ventriloquists are known for working with one particular partner, some like Jeff Dunham and Terry Fator have multiple figure and add new ones to there show on a regular basis. Jeff Dunham also has a three way section with Peanut and Jose but for most of the time it's going to be you and a side kick, or should that be the other way around as it is normally the ventriloquist who plays the straight man.

One English ventriloquist of note was Arthur Worsley, he had a unique take on the ventriloquial art, he used to remain almost silent throughout his act whist being heckled by his side kick Charlie Brown. Charlie would keep trying to get him to repeat difficult sayings such as "bottle of beer" etc whilst starring at Arthur trying to see if his mouth moved! Although you are a double act, the great thing about being a ventriloquist is that you get to keep all the money!

The downside for some people is that they will always be playing second fiddle to their partner. Some ventriloquists get fed up with people asking where their partner is and all the attention being for the puppet. I often get calls asking if I am Snot the Dragon! At the end of the day the cheques are made out in my name!

If you are a magician performing children's shows then ventriloquism is a great way of adding variety to your act. Children love to see a funny looking puppet getting the better of the magician. It is also fairly easy to get the puppet to do some magic tricks. Most of my puppets do a magic trick or two, I feel if I have talking animals they might as well do a trick as well!

Where can I work?

First you have to decide on your main audience group, are you going to be performing more for adults or for children. It is harder to find an audience for an adult show, especially in the UK. If you want to perform for children then there is a much bigger market with birthday parties and Christmas shows. In addition to birthday parties if you can get a show to fit a specific educational topic you could perform on weekdays in schools, or during the school holiday there is work at holiday camps. Most of the music festivals have kids areas and this is a good way of getting into a festival for free and picking up a bit of extra money too, you won't earn the same as you would for a full weekend of birthday parties but when you consider the price of admission to a festival, and the fact that you will be finished working long before the headline acts come on, it can be a fun weekend. Another advantage of festivals is that you will get to work for a large number of children and get to promote your self to a larger audience.

If you want to perform for adults then your main markets are going to be holiday camps and comedy clubs. If you are working in a standard comedy club then it can be hard for an audience to get used to seeing a puppet on stage, but saying that, I perform at several comedy clubs with routines that are almost straight from my kids show and they go down well.

Another good market for ventriloquists are cruise ships. These ships have some of the finest theatres you will find, seating up to a thousand people! You will need to have two different 45 minute shows for most ships. These shows should ideally be suitable for a family audience as although you might be booked as an "adult" act there is a good possibility that there will be some youngsters in the audience and you don't want to offend anyone on board.

Cruises have some very specific guidelines and if these aren't followed to the letter you can quickly find yourself being removed from the ship. On the other hand if the cruise director likes you, it can mean multiple bookings as the audience will change every two weeks. You will have to be prepared to spend a long time away from home and you'll have to like travel. Cruise companies work from ports all around the world, if they like your act you can be asked to fly almost anywhere in the world to catch a ship for a week. Some entertainers make a very good living without doing any shows on dry land.

How To Start?

I got my start in ventriloquism by accident. I was performing as a magician in children's shows, I had bought a new prop fora show but when it arrived I was very disappointed so I decided to change it. I went to the Magic Circle dealers day to see the dealer I bought it from to see what else they had on offer, the only thing they had that appealed to me was an Axtell Pedro Parrot, I bought it thinking I could start by just giving it a squawk or two but over the next few months I learnt more about how to addwords to my script and he joined the show, when I realised how much the children enjoyed him I was hooked.

Basic Ventriloquism.

The science of ventriloquism.

I was asked a few years ago to be the ventriloquist on the "Discovery Channel's Amazing Body Parts program". On the program which was about eyes and ears they talked about the science of ventriloquism. One of the reasons that ventriloquism is an effective illusion is down to the fact that our eyes are a more dominant force than our ears, this means that if a sound is coming from one source but a movement that corresponds with that sound is coming from another, the brain will be fooled in to thinking that the sound is coming from where the movement is. This works especially well for ventriloquism because the figure is not that far from the source of the sound and of course if you are using a microphone then all the sound comes from the same set of speakers.

How hard is this ventriloquism lark?

The thing about talking without moving your lips is that most of the alphabet is easy, the vowels are all easy, give it a go, A.E.I.O.U. even the rest of the alphabet is easier than you would think.

A C D E G H I J K L N O Q R S T U X Y Z

That just leaves B F M P V W

So what do we do about them? Well the easiest thing to do is to try and avoid them, you can do this by either writing scripts that don't use the difficult letters, this is easier than you would imagine, if you get stuck for a replacement word, check out a thesaurus, it might make the rest of your script more interesting. But if you truly want to be a ventriloquist then you have to learn how to do the difficult bits.

How to do the hard bits.

Most of the hard letters can be replaced with similar sounding letters lets look at each one in turn.

B & P

The standard substitution for the letter B is D so instead of saying, "The boy likes bananas", you would say "The doy likes dananas"

The standard substitution for P is T so "tractise make terfect"

The most important part of these replacements is to think of the actual letter whilst you are saying the replacement sound so that although you are saying dananas, you must think bananas, in doing this you will find you get a much more realistic sounds coming out, your mouth can do some amazing tricks.

Put your tongue against your top teeth, now bring it back a bit and you will find the alveolar ridge. Play around with popping sounds using your tongue on you teeth and on the ridge. Try saying B words and P words using the substitutions and figure out what works best for you.

F & V

Both F and V get replaced by a th sound "His friend bought him a very nice present" becomes "His thriend dought him a thery nice tresent"

l with an N or an ng sound as in singing. So "His
ery nice present for his mother" becomes "His
thery nice tresent for his ngother" Give it a go, see

I learnt my basic technique from the free information available on the
Axtell Expressions web site, www.axtell.com/learn.html from there I
played around with my technique to find something that worked for
me. The funny thing with Bs and Ps is, we think they are difficult to
say because they require a lot of lip movement but what do you expect
a parrot, that talks to say? "Polly want a cracker" and "Who's a pretty
boy then?" Lots of Bs and Ps and parrots don't even have lips! How
do they do it, well they use their tongues to stop the air, to make the
harsh sounds and thats exactly what we have to do.

Remember the syllables.

The mouth of your partner should open with every syllable, its always worth while having a look at your own mouth reading your partners script to see exactly how your mouth opens and closes. The better the synchronisation between your partners words and mouth movement the better the illusion. You don't want to look like a badly dubbed movie!

Tom Crowl with Dangerous a Pavlov Duck

Further Instruction.

For a full course on ventriloquism I recommend you go to Tom Crowl's web site. http://www.learn-ventriloquism.com This a fantastic course with 36 high definition video lessons.

There is also a new revamped Maher Studio ventriloquist course. The Maher course has been going for years and some of the top ventriloquists, especially in the USA got started with this course.

Just like most things in life, you don't need to be special to do ventriloquism you just need to have the motivation to practice, and that might come in the form of a new puppet!A script with all the letters!

Here's a little piece I put together for a reading show for schools, it's not the easiest script I have but it's worth having a look at.

Script about letters

Me.   This is Alfie Bates

Figure What are you doing?

M: We're going to do our alphabet.

F: I got an auntie Bette.

M: No the alphabet, Its all the letters in the correct place.

F: My uncle does that.

M: What?

F: He's a postman.

M: No, not those kind of letters! These are the ones we use for making words.

F   Can you teach me?

M: You want to learn the alphabet?

F: Yeah where do we start?

M: A.

F: I said where do we start, and it's pardon not A.

M: No A is the first letter of the alphabet.

F: Oh!

M: No not O, O is the 15th letter.

F: Eh!

M: Yes A!

F: I'm confused.

m: Just listen. A B.

F: It's a story about a bee, I like Bees they make hunny.

M: Not that kind of bee. B is the second letter.

F: Oh!

M: No not O that's the fifteenth.

F: Eh!

M: That's the start now listen. A B C D

F: The Bee had a recording contract!

M   Noo it's not a Bee. Will you please let me get to the end

F   I don't know why you keep stopping.

M   ABCDEFGHIJKLMNOP

F   Now you mention it.

M   What?

F   Pee. I need to go.

M   You'll have to wait, cross your legs.(*Cross Floyd's legs*)

      I'll start again from the beginning. Maybe the children can

      help me. A-Z

F   Wow is that it.

M   What do you mean is that it.

F   Well there are all these books and they're all made with just

      those few letters.

M   Yep 26 letters is all you need.

F   Can I have ago

M	Do you think you can.
F	I don't know about the wasp.
M	The Bee
F	That's easy for you to say! and the figure(*looks down*)
M	Get on with it.
F	A
M	I said get on with it.
F	I had. A-Z
M	Give him a clap. well done.
F	Hey I bet I can do it backwards.
M	That takes a lot of practice.
F	No I can do it. Watch.(*turns around*) A-Z.
M	Stop that.
F	Just joking. I'll do it properly.
M	If you can do that we'll give you a real big round of applause.
F	Here goes. (*coughs*) zyxwvutsrqponmlkjihgfedcba

How to choose a puppet!

Yeah, here comes the fun bit!

Slow down tiger, there are a few things to think about before you go and buy a new puppet.

Question one: Hard or Soft?

There are two main types of puppets for ventriloquism, Hard figures, some people get upset if you call them "dummies" but I don't care, the traditional name for a vent figure in the UK is Doll, I'd rather play with dummies than with dolls! Then there are soft figures, often called puppets and there is a wide variation for both soft and hard figures!

Hard Figure

Hard figures tend to be human style figures with a whole range of movements available, all come with moving mouths, you'd be a funny looking ventriloquist if your friends mouth never moved! then you can add side to side moving eyes, closing and wide eyes either one control or separate controls so the figure can blink! up and down eyebrows, upper lip sneer, waggling ears, lifting wig, sticking out tongue, lighting up nose, spitting, crying, and I'm sure there are more that I haven't thought about. These are all worked from a head stick via brass rods or pieces of string!

The most expensive of hard figures are hand carved from bass wood, this is the traditional American figure, modern figures can be made from various "like wood' compounds and can be moulded rather than carved. The traditional British figure is made from papier mache. The other main difference in British figures is the mouth movements, American figures have a slot jaw whereas the British figures have what is called a living mouth, this is a moving lower lip where the gap is covered in leather to make a more natural finish.

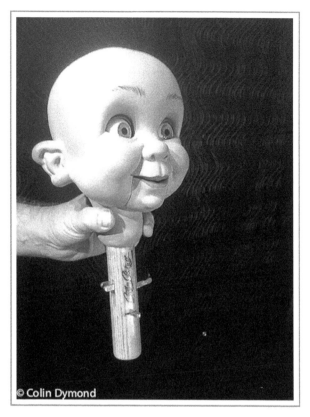

Tim Selberg "Tater" figure
Right hand controls, Thumb-mouth, middle finger-
side to side eyes, Index finger blinkers.

Hard figures are fine for an adult audience but children, and some adults, find them quite scary! I think it's all those horror movies!

The other problem with hard figures is that they can be quite delicate, if a string breaks or a rod becomes disconnected you can end up with a puppet that wont talk! Even worse, if you drop your figure it could just shatter and hard figures are not cheap! A good quality figure with minimal movement will set you back a month's wages!

Care of hard figures.

The best place for your hard figure is in a custom case, these are often made by the person who built the puppet. Foam can be added to a suitcase and cut to size so your figure sits snugly in its protective cocoon. The head, hands and feet if your figure has them should always be kept covered in something soft and protective. I use socks for the hands and feet and a padded bag for the head.

Noted Builders

• Tim Selberg

• Conrad Hartz, hand carved basswood

• Albert Alfaro

• Geoff Felix, Insull style paper mache

• James Jimmy Eisenberg: Papier Mache

A Tim Selberg, Rupert Figure

Soft Figures

Soft figures come in just about every size and shape imaginable, from small hand puppets to large arm puppets, they can be people or animals and can be made from various materials including foam, latex or fabric. Although they tend not to have too many extra features you can get a lot of facial expression because the face and mouth tends to be quite pliable. Other features that can be added include closing eyes, raising ears, my dragon has flapping wings and the ability to shoot Snot from his nose, the initial intention was for him to breathe smoke but Snot was funnier.

One of the most famous ventriloquists to use a soft figure was Shari Lewis who had Lamb Chop as her main figure, Lamb Chop was basically a sock with some arms and legs stuck on. Soft figures have been making quite a comeback in recent times and are probably seen more often than hard figures, Jeff Dunham has Peanut, Nina Conti has Monk, Paul Zerdin has Sam and Terry Fator has a whole host of soft figures.

The advantage of soft figures is that they are cheaper to buy, easier to look after, lighter to transport and can be a lot friendlier looking so less scary for children or adults who watch too many scary movies!

If you don't want to mess up your socks, the next cheapest option is a small hand puppet with a moving mouth, these can be bought in toy shops for the price of a cup of coffee and a cake!

Probably the biggest maker of soft puppets is Axtell Expressions, my first professional puppet was their parrot, I have since bought loads more. Steve Axtell makes a huge range from birds to full size animatronic talking trees! Axtell Expressions are know for their latex faces, these allows for lots of movement and so greater expressions than are available with a foam mouthed puppet.

If you use a bird puppet or any other creature that just covers your forearm then the Axtell bird arm illusion is well worth investing in. This devise is a false arm covered in a glove that gives the illusion that the bird is sitting on your out stretched arm, this is a great illusion that can be viewed from all angles.

Axtell Hands Free Lite

Various "staging" options available with Hands Free Lite

Axtell Expression make a range of animatronic puppets from a huge talking tree to their hands-free lite system, this allows a small arm puppet to fit on the stand and then using the controller you can make it's head turn from side to side and it's mouth to open. You can have a parrot in a cage or a possum sat on a box as you can build things around the basic structure.

Foam based puppets.

Think Muppet, foam based puppets are normally full arm puppets where, for ventriloquists, your arm enters the back of the puppets, if you were doing standard puppetry with the puppeteer under the desk their hand would enter from the bottom of the puppet. Some foam puppets are made from a pattern of foam pieces being glued together to form the shape before being covered in whatever material is needed to give the character its final look. Other puppets, including Snot the Dragon are carved from a piece of hard foam before being covered in material, this is great for getting added detail but the downside is that because there is no pattern if you need a replacement the builder will need your puppet back to do a re-sculpt.

Mark Wade with his ,MAT Gorilla and Puppet Planet
Bird

Care of soft puppets.

Because they are soft they can be quite forgiving but remember not to squash them too much as they might not regain their original shape! If you are travelling with soft puppets stuff their insides with t-shirts to keep the shape. Keep them in soft bags or pillowcases to stop them getting dirty. Always have clean hands when operating a puppet and try not to touch their face. Latex puppets should be treated with a special cleaner to keep them looking their best and prolongs the life of the latex.

With a little care your soft puppet should give you years of fun.

Noted Builders

Toy Puppets:- Folkmanis, The Puppet Company

- Latex:- Axtell Expressions
- Foam:- MAT puppets, Jet, Pavlov.
- Custom Builds, Darryl Worbey(Colin Dymond, Paul Zerdin),
- Peter Pullon (Steve Hewlett, Jimmy Tamely)
    - Mat (Mark Wade)
    - Axtell (Terry Fator)

Custom Made Figures.

So you've looked at all the "stock" figures from all the makers and can't quite find what you are looking for or you just want something that is yours, what are your options. Well, if you

Lolly my Custom Axtell Parrot

want a true original figure, it's going to cost you serious money, I think the rule of thumb is to look at what a figure makers standard price is and then add a 0 to the end! All the ventriloquists that you have heard of have some kind of original figure but there are other ways of having some originality without all the costs. You could just add your own clothing to it, this is great for hard figures as they take standard children's clothes with a bit of thought you can really add character to your partner at very little cost.

With soft figures it is often possible to have them made in a different material for a small extra cost. I had Steve Axtell make a version of his Pedro Parrot for me in my corporate colours, he also gave her different wings, she now looks unlike any parrot Steve has made, but she didn't cost an arm and a leg!

Steve Hewlett with ChiChi made by Peter Pullon

My dragon on the other hand is a completely different affair. After years of using standard figures and dealing with children saying "I know him" when pointing at my puppet, I made the decision that I was going to get my own character made. After a lot of searching, I decided to go with a British maker, Darryl Worbey, that way I could meet up with him during the consultation and at set times during the build.

The star of my show Snot the Dragon
Made by Darryl Worbey

The build process started with me explaining to Darryl my thoughts about the size of puppet I wanted and describing his character. Darryl then did some sketches and I chose the ones that appealed to me the most. Then there was the choice of fabric, I went for purple fur with a yellow tummy and green wings. I met up with Darryl a couple of times during the build to check on sizes, especially for wings as they wanted to be big enough to be seen from the back of the hall but not too big as they would get in my way. One of the most important fittings was to get the mouth plate right for my hand, he is a perfect fit, so much so that when I tried to use him on my left hand, so I could use another puppet on my right, he didn't fit at all! I now have my own main character, Snot the Dragon and he goes on all my publicity and is better known than me!

Four years after the initial build, I went back to Darryl to see about changing the wings for ones that flap, this has been a great addition to him as it has added extra character and gags.

David Tomkins and Cheeky Dog
Cheeky Dog was made by Darryl Worbey

Not quite puppets.

There are several things that we can use as a ventriloquist that aren't quite puppets, some people use split tennis balls and paint a face on them to make a puppet, Jay Marshall used to paint a face onto his hand and used his thumb as the mouth. These are great ideas but there are more options you can invest in to add a different character to your show.

Magic Drawing Board

Steve Axtell with the original Magic Drawing

This is a great invention by Steve Axtell, he doesn't claim to be the inventor of a talking picture, that goes so far back that no one knows who did that first but what Steve came up with was a reliable, reusable board that you could draw a face on and then have it come to life with moving eyes and a moving mouth.

The reaction you get to this when it comes to life is amazing. I use mine in various ways but the way I use it the most is by drawing really bad pictures of various audience members before I finally draw a picture of me. I then tell the audience that you can always tell a good picture because the eyes follow you around the room, I then move the eyes without seeing them move myself. After I notice the eyes move, I say "hey" and the pictures says "hey" back, in my voice, I then tell the audience that not only does it look like me but it sounds like me too.

Axtell expression make a hands free version of the board which is great as you can move away from the picture and still have it talk, this is great if you start off holding it so the audience think they know how it works and then you walk away!

The newest version of the Magic Drawing Board has a sticking out tongue! Everyone loves a sticking out tongue.

Vent Mask.

Again this is a very old concept that has found new life in the last few years. A vent mask is a mask with a moving mouth that you can put on a spectator so you can take over his voice.

The simplest ones have a length of string hanging from the lower jaw and are operated just by pulling the string, the more complex ones have a bicycle brake lever arrangement where you pull the lever and the cable operates the mouth.

Peter Pullon Ventriloquist Mask

If you pick the right audience volunteer you will get laughs right from the start, but you still need a good script otherwise the laughs will soon dry up! Also the selection of your volunteer is very important, you want to find someone who looks like they are having fun but not the person who wants to be centre of attention. If you have "the life and soul of the party" up to help they will try to take over the stage and make your job a lot harder, if you pick a "shrinking violet" you won't get enough out of them to make the routine funny. In a comedy club or cabaret situation try and find someone who is there with several friends that way their friends will be the first to laugh and will set the tone for the piece, if you pick someone who is there on their own or just with a partner you run the risk of the section being very flat. Do not be tempted to go along with anyone else's suggestions as to who would be "perfect" know your own mind about the type of person who will fit your routine.

The demon drink! Do not pick someone who has been drinking! Sometimes it's hard to tell in a club how much someone has been drinking so be safe, see if you can spot the designated driver, the one with a coke in front of them, they are a much safer bet than someone who when you get them on stage you realise that they can hardly stand up and won't want to corporate in anything you need them to do. You have been warned!!!

Mic Mouth

This is another great invention by Steve Axtell. The problem with a vent mask is that it needs to be strapped to the volunteers face, this is great because it means the mask is going to stay where you want it but for some people they can find it claustrophobic, it's also not suitable to use with children, so Steve came up with the idea of a mouth at the end of a microphone. The workings are simple, all you have to do is to place the mouth in front of your helpers mouth and you open and close it my a lever at the back of the microphone. This is also great if you want to do a game show routine with numerous contestants on stage. You can along a row of helpers asking them questions and supplying the answers you could have the last person in line never

saying anything, or just saying pass!

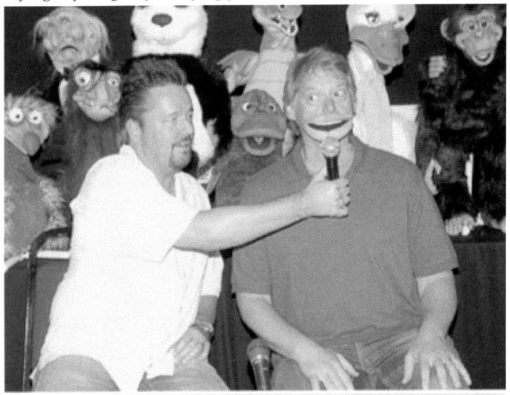

Terry Fator uses Mic Mouth on it's creator Steve Axtell

How to avoid buying puppets that you won't use!

This might be the most important chapter in the book!!!

Every person I know who is into their puppets has spent a small fortune on puppets that never get to perform in a show, they go to a convention or a puppet shop, see a great looking puppet and buy it with no idea what they are going to do with it, "it will be great" they say, "I'm sure I'll find a use for it!" Then it sits on a shelf and every now again it might get taken down and played with before it gets put back on the shelf.

These are just my Axtell puppets!!!

you go looking for a puppet, know what you are going to use it for! Or if you see a puppet that you like, see if you can come up with ten jokes or scenarios that could work with it before you put it on your arm, once it's gone on your arm you are done for!

Be flexible, if you have a great script for an old man, what other type of puppet might it fit with, maybe a big, gruff looking bear, or even a lion! If you script if for a shy young girl maybe it would fit with any baby animal.

"But I'm no good at writing scripts!" Well you best skip along to the next chapter for some help then!

How to Write a Script

Where do you start when writing a script?

Do not "borrow" anyone else's material, I know it's easy and there are so many "bits" that are as old as the hills and are almost considered "Public Domain" as they are so well know, "where's your hand?" etc. that no one knows who said them first but if you use them, they might get a laugh but the audience will probably have heard them too. When it comes to other peoples routines then that is a complete no no, unless they have been published in script books on DVDs intended for other people's use. I have a DVD, The Magic of Puppets that has a couple of full routines that you can use. There are also several script books available and there are the great scripts put out by Maher Studios that give you a full audio version so you can learn all about timing. When using material that you have not written please at least go through it and make sure it makes sense coming from your mouth in your accent.

Keep a notebook with you at all times! Comedians, and you do want your scripts to be funny don't you?, keep note books with them at all times, you never know when you will see something funny, or have an idea pop in your head. In fact we all carry notebooks with us now, they are called phones. Your smart phone comes with a notebook, a voice recorder and even dictation software so really there is no excuse for not getting those thoughts down. It's a good idea to then organise your notes when you get home and tag them with topics, that way you can find those gems when you need them.

Form a writing circle. What's one of those? well just get together with some friends, hopefully those that are funny and start writing together. Pick a topic say, "the zoo" then fire off as many things that might be funny about a trip to the zoo. Don't filter anything!!! Normally the first stuff that comes out will be far too rude to put in your show but get that out of the way and you can then concentrate on the next level stuff. The more ideas you get out the more good ones will be there. The more often you meet the more ideas you will get out and the more you get in the swing of things the better the results will be. Try to find people with different interests to be in your group. If you are all performers you are going to have to decide who gets to keep what lines. We all like to think that our ideas are funny enough on our own but take a look at the writing credits on your favourite show or on a comedians DVD and you will see that there is actually a big team of writers involved.

Are we there yet?

You have your puppet friend, you have a script, are you ready to hit the stage.

NO!

If you go on stage now there will just be two versions of your self talking to each other! You partner needs a character!

How to create a character

Trying out an Axtell Small Bear

One of the best ways to create a character for your friend is to write a back story for him. This should contain as much information as possible.

Here is my character development for snot the Dragon

Basics

Name:- Sir Nigel of Trelawney SNOT for short

Sex:- Boy

Age:- 5 in Dragon years but 51, the same as me in human years.

Place of Birth: He was left as an egg at my Dads small farm in North Cornwall

Where he lives now: In Stroud with me in a tree house

Does he have a job: No still at Dragon School, still learning to fly.

Special Talent: Fires Snot, young Dragons can't breath fire!

What is his wider Family: He has no siblings but he has an Aunty who lives in a far off forest. He is from an ancient order of Cornish Dragons

Physical Characteristics:

These tend to be decided by the puppet if it is a stock puppet but are a good idea to have listed before you go shopping.

I wanted Snot to have small horns, a long tail and a plumpish body. he also had to be purple!

Mannerisms:

Habits: Likes to flap his wings in my face and fire snot at me.

Health: Eats too much chocolate and custard.

Hobbies: Flying, it's his new thing.

Favorite Sayings: Smelly Socks in Custard

Speech patterns: Quite excited, slight Cornish accent but tries to speak properly. High pitched young boy.

Disabilities: None

Style (Elegant, shabby etc.): Doesn't care

Greatest flaw: Me

Best quality: Wants to help.

Schools:

Dragons don't do school. He goes sometimes

Intelligence Level: Average

Learning Experiences: Still Flying, he's eaten a few things he shouldn't have!

What does he want to be when he grows up: Fireman!

What would most embarrass him: Girls

You can add more to your list especially if you are doing school shows on a theme. How does your character feel about Animals, recycling, the environment, bullies, maths etc.

We are now making progress.

Giving your puppet a voice.

So you know all about your new friend but he still has no voice, where do you find one? Have you looked under the sofa? No!

Where to start. Sing a scale starting from as low as you can, to as high as you can without going into falsetto, don't worry about hitting the right notes, this is just to get an idea of your range.

Ok let's put a bit of a chart together

	Low	Mid	High	Falsetto
Slow	Clint Eastwood			Dame Edna
Mid		Lord Charles		
Fast			Peanut	
Super Fast			Auctioneer	

Try filling in some of the gaps, I've filled a few voices for you.

So you now have 30 different types of voices if you added just 5 distinct character traits e.g. Cool, Not so bright, Posh, Old, Childish, you now have 150 different voices. What are you like with accents? Cockney, New York, Southern American, Australian, French, Italian, Scottish, Yokel, Russian, Scandinavian, we now have 1500 different voices! Don't try them all in one show!

Lets look at some possibilities

If we go for a slow and low voice with a cool character and an American accent and start thinking Clint Eastwood

Try a mid range and a mid speed give him a posh accent and think Tim, Nice but Dim.

Mid Low. This with a bit of speed can give you a great Cockney Geezer, add a bit of a growl to the voice and try the accent. Be careful with accents that are hard on the throat, only do them for a short time or you could cause damage!

Oscar my Axtell Orang-Utan is the star of "The Living Planet"
an environmental awareness show for schools.

Women's voices should in general be done in your high, normal range and not into the falsetto, I am taking about men here but… Falsetto is more for a comedy voice, very few humans speak that high.

My favourite place for inspiration for voices is from old cartoons, don't try to do an impression of that character but just get a feel for it. Look at where you'd place the character on the grid, then the accent and any speech patterns that they have. cartoons often have exaggerated stutters or lisps or mis pronunciations, you can take a speech pattern and add it to another voice.

The choices are endless, if you think about it, you can tell who's on the phone just from their voice even, people from the same town and same family all have something different about them. With all these different voice options available try your best to make your puppet voices different from yours and different from each other.

Practice the voice without worrying about lip control but don't perfect it yet. try your new voice with lip control, some accents are easier to do than others and what works for you might not work for everyone.

We are nearly there!

It's Alive!

How to bring your partner to life!

Good Manipulation is the difference between having a living partner or a dead doll.

There are several "Golden Rules

1.   Keep It Alive

2.   Keep it Natural

3.   Treat as real

4.   Remember Gravity

5.   Thumb tip

6.   Keep your emotions separate.

Lets take a look at each of these in turn.

Keep it alive.

From the moment your sidekick makes his entrance until the moment he is put away he should always be alive. So what do I mean by alive? I mean that he should always be moving, looking around, reacting to what you are saying or to what the audie54 nce is doing. If you watch Dan Horn, his old man figure, Orson is always flirting with someone to his side of the stage while Dan is trying to talk. Like all good double acts, it's a one at a time thing, the partner is always doing something. Listening is not a passive state, if you a good listener you will be nodding making a few interjections.

Keep it natural

When your friend is not talking it should be moving but don't over exaggerate this movement. I have seen some ventriloquists who's partner looks like it's in desperate need for the toilet or it's on a bouncy castle, bobbing up and down with it's head swivelling from side to side. Slow it down, keep it real!

Treat as Real

I tend to use a side table or a vent stand for my friend to sit on, one of the reasons for this is for a start it gives me a hand free for handling magic props and gives my puppet more freedom of movement. I have seen too many people get a puppet and literally shove it into their arm pit so they can hold it, this looks wrong and mean! This is meant to be your friend. One of the best example to think about is how would you hold a pet. If you had a dog the size of a sheepdog you wouldn't shove him under your arm, if you had a Chihuahua you might have him in a small bag so why not put it in a bag, maybe with a false hand at the front to make it look like you are holding him. If it's a rabbit then why not have him in a top hat? You can make a hole in the back of the hat for your hand to go through and again have a false hand on the bottom of the hat. Ventriloquism is an illusion so why not make it the best illusion it can be by not giving the audience some concept to struggle with. I have already talked about the Axtell bird arm illusion, this doesn't just have to be for birds, any creature that will fit and still looks natural is worth trying. The Axtell hands free lite system allows you to put some of its smaller puppets on it so you can operate them by remote control, this is a fantastic illusion and would work particularly well if you wanted a third partner on stage with you.

Remember Gravity.

One of my absolute pet hates when watching people with puppets is to see the puppet suspended in mid air, to me it just kills the illusion. Your partner is supposed to be real and as such is affected by all the physical forces that you and I are effected by. Give your puppet a sense of weight, when he stands on a table it should look like he is standing, not floating above it. A good idea would be to have some lessons in mime, that's a great way to learn about physical forces that are not actually there and help you to move your puppet correctly. Study animals and people to see what they can and can't do. Watch the difference between a puppy and an old dog, see how people change with time. One of my favourite ventriloquists, Ray Alan, had his figure, Lord Charles, age as he got older. The puppet had a few more lines and his hair started to go grey just enough to keep the performer and partner with similar age gap as they had in the beginning. A nice touch in keeping it real!

Thumb Tip

This only applies to soft figures. When opening and shutting the mouth of a soft puppet it is your thumb that should be doing the work and not your fingers, if you start to move your fingers you just have a puppet with a flappy head, animals and humans don't do that, we have a bottom jaw that is designed for moving and a stationary head. This can feel quite awkward at first but it needs to be put into practice form the start so you don't get into bad habits.

A good way of thinking about forming the words if you think that you are trying to push them out from the back of the puppets mouth, you are pushing the words towards the audience. Sometimes you see a puppet that looks wrong when it is talking, it looks like the puppet is snapping at the words, trying to eat them.

Snot has flying lessons!

Keep your emotions separate.

This is one of the hardest things to do when talking to your self and you will need to spend some time practicing in the mirror and watching videos of your performances and practice sessions. You are meant to be reacting to what has been said and not preempting it. If the audience see you look amused as your partner is telling a joke then it will look wrong. In language it is said that only 7% of the meaning is actually the words that come out of mouths the other 93% is body language, facial expressions and the tone of voice. We have spent our whole lives using body language and facial expressions to add to the words, now when we do ventriloquism not only do we have to switch them off, we have to use the body language and facial express that go along with listening to what is coming out from our partners mouths. One thing you can do to help this is to record your partners voice and play that back whilst you watch your expressions in a mirror, you can then do it the other way around and concentrate on how your partner should react to everything you are saying. And you thought rubbing your tummy and patting your head was difficult.

Watch your emotions

How can you get a piece of wood or a rag doll to convey real emotions?

Depending on the type of figure you are using will depend on what emotions you can portray and how you go about it.

Hard Figure; The best movement on a hard figure to show emotions is raising and lowering eyebrows. From surprise to anger and most stops in between. Closing eyes can add a level of boredom, distain, wide eyes add to the surprise or fear. An upper lip sneer movement not only adds a sneer but can also be a wide grin.

Soft Figure; My favourite thing to do to get emotions for soft, animal puppets is to watch other animals, dogs are especially easy to see what they are thinking. A dog with his mouth open and a spring in his step is a happy lively dog as he gets more nervous he will sink down into himself and be more on the back foot. A curious dog will have his head on one side another great addition to your emotional repertoire is the sniff! Move the dog's head forward and as you sniff give him a sharp backward move of the head, this is how a lot of animals get to know their surroundings.

Another device that can help to convey various emotions is the use of a rod arm. A rod arm can be a rod that fits inside the puppets arm from the wrist and comes out by the elbow, this allows you to use small movements at the elbow and get larger movement at the puppets hand. Some ventriloquists like to use long rods that connect to the puppets wrists, check out Dan Horn to see amaster of this type of maipulation. Rod arms can be fitted to either hard or soft figures and can be used simply to point or you can suggest shame, with the hand over the eyes, laughter if you hold the puppets belly as it rocks backward and forwards. We all use our hads to add to communication, think what you can add to your puppets vocabulary with a little practice.

Apes are another good sours of emotional education, there are lots of videos online to see how they behave in different situation.

Be observant of people and pets and your emotion and manipulation will get better. You need to keep practicing and keep videoing your sessions. Be critical, you will never get better if you think "that will do

Where do you go from here?

So you now have a basic script, some realistic movements from your partner, a good voice that is different from your own, it's Show Time!

Show Time

When I first added ventriloquism to my act, I only did it in shows for the younger children, my logic behind this was that they wouldn't be so critical and the fact that there was a magic, talking parrot should be enough to distract them from my less than perfect lip control. I was booked to do a large first birthday party, first birthdays are a huge family event for some communities and there were children of all ages there, I decided I would "go for it" and do my parrot routine for everybody, if the older kids saw through the illusion there would be something more in the age range in other parts of my show. I was very surprised at the end of the show when a group of boys, aged between 9-11 came up to ask how the parrot worked. They said they totally understood how it worked until it started talking to them directly and mentioning them by name and making reference to what they were wearing. What I had failed to notice was that unlike when I was young, when there were several ventriloquists on TV but all your toys were mute, in the early 2000s there were no ventriloquists on TV but several children's toys would communicate with the children, some could even be set off by sensors as the children walked into their rooms. From that moment on my parrot routine was in every show and just like anything, the more I did it the better it became. I soon added more puppet friends into my show and it is now almost a 50-50 mix of magic and ventriloquism.

Start with an easy, funny script that you feel relatively confident in and just bite the bullet and go for it.

If you are doing pure ventriloquism i.e. just you and your partner talking, I would suggest you keep these routines fairly short if you are working for children. My particular specialty, is getting my puppets to perform a magic trick often with the help of an audience member, if you are doing this then you can lengthen the piece. Never pad your scripts out to extend a routine, if anything you should be constantly editing your scripts to get rid of any fluff so you are hitting as many laughs per minute as you can.

Stage Set Up

For my children's shows I have two flight cases both of which are at the right height for me to comfortably sit a puppet on. A good working height is one where your eyes are slightly higher than your puppets but the main thing is that you should be comfortable so you are not stretching up or leaning over, if you are going to be doing this for a long time you will soon end up with a bad back if you are working at the wrong height. With my set up, the flight case to my right is like a suitcase with a lid that opens out towards the audience, this is home to Snot the Dragon, this means I can get Snot out of case with the lid hiding how I actually get into the puppet. The set up to my left is actually two cases set one on top of the other, these have removable backs so they are open towards the back of the stage, this too hides how I get into the puppets.

When I am working comedy clubs I often take my puppets in a holdall and just have a vent stand to work from. One point I would make about working from a holdall is to make sure there is enough room so that you can get your friend on your arm as quickly as possible and if you are using more than one puppet that there is room to put one away with out it getting in the way of the second puppet that you need to get out. No one wants to watch you mess around trying to get your puppets on and off!

Think about how you will be transporting your partners and where you are performing, a tatty holdall might look fine in a comedy club but a posh case will look more professional if you are working a smart cabaret or a cruise liner. If you are going to fly with your puppets, this is especially the case if you are working cruises and they need you to pick up a cruise in a different country, you will need to think about weight. There are some great lightweight cases such as Peli that are incredibly strong, but they don't come cheap.

Being heard.

So you now have a great show and a cool looking set up and everything packs away nice and neat, one last piece of the jigsaw, you need to be heard!

My rule with your sound equipment is to buy the best you can, it's no good having a great show if no one can hear you. A PA system that has more power than you need can be turned down, a PA system that is not up to the job will distort and make you sound bad. If you have bad sound it makes it very hard for the audience to concentrate and all they will remember if that it sounded horrible.

In the last few years the quality and range of small, portable PA systems has left the older style systems way behind. If you are doing birthday parties or school shows they will expect you to bring your own PA, if you are doing comedy clubs or theatres they should have their own systems.

My choice of system for the last few year was HK Audio Lucas Nano 300 £598.00p

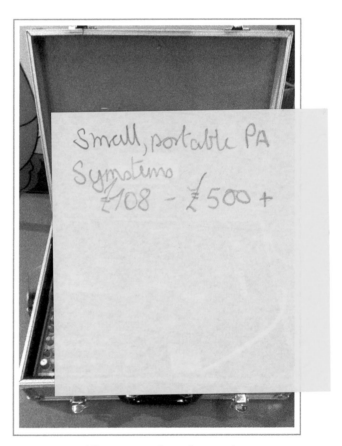

Small, portable PA Systems
£108 – £500 +

All set up and ready to go!
Note the iPad running Show Cues

In my set up I have a case with a four way extension lead with my radio mic and charger for my iPad plus the power for my Lucas Nano. I then have the output leads from the radio mic, and my iPad plus the power lead for the Nano cable tied together so that when I get to the venue I just have one "snake" to plug in.

The Nano consists of one unit that holds the amp and the subwoofer, very cleverly attached in a recess in the back are the two satellite speakers for the mid high speakers. There are a few ways to set up the Nano, the satellite speakers can be kept together and slotted on top of the main unit, this is idea in a house party, you can get an extra pole to raise the height of the satellites for better projection.

My set up of choice is the full stereo option using an additional stand and having the two satellite speakers either side of me on stage, this fills the room with sound all the way to the back of the hall.

The Nano 300 is suitable for most shows that a children's entertainer would do but I am now using the HK Audio Lucas Nano 600.

The 600 is like the 300 on steroids, it's bigger and beefier doubling the size of the power amp from 230watts to 460 watts.

The great thing about the Nano is that because it is a stereo system with directional satellite speakers you can really focus the sound where you need it. The 600 will cope effortlessly for most shows where you bring your own PA and its quick and easy to set up in less than 5 minutes!

If you really need more oomph then you can link two systems together!

HK Audio Lucas Nano 600

If you are spending good money on your PA system you will also need to spend money on a good quality microphone. I use a DA capo D12 microphone, this is a discrete headset microphone, it is very lightweight, I can wear it for a whole show and forget that I have it on. The advantage of a headset mic is that it moves with you so you have a constant volume. If you are working in clubs you might have to use their hand held mic so it is worthwhile practicing with one to get you technique right, you need to know where you mouth needs to be in relation to the microphone. Some vents in the past have used a big microphone to hide bad technique but you are going to better than that, aren't you?

Music

My puppets have their own "play on" music and I also use some sound effects, these are controlled by an app on my iPad called Show Cues, I use a remote control, that can be operated by an ankle switch, to change between tracks. You can set up the tracks with delayed starts and fade outs if needed, it's a great bit of kit to give your performance a more professional feel.

Marketing Your Show

So you now have a show but you can't really call your self a ventriloquist if you are not performing for real people in a show. Where are you going to perform if no one knows about you and you don't have tried and tested material? You don't want to turn up before a paying audience if your only audience has been a mirror or your family, I'll let you in to a secret, both the mirror and your friends lie! It is amazing how much you can ignore when working in front of a mirror or even watching a video playback, there is a great way of finding out magicians who practice in front of mirrors, they blink when they do the 'move" so they never spot how bad they are!

It's hard for your family to tell you if you suck! They love you, a live audience don't have to be so nice!

Your first gigs will probably be free shows.

Free Shows?

Who will let me work fro free? A lot of pubs have open mic nights, these are normally for singers and musicians but they often like to have a bit of variety in them, if you do a few for the same pub you will see if you are getting better as hopefully you will get more laughs every time you appear. The other option is comedy clubs, the standard formula for small comedy clubs in the UK is that they have an MC, then an opening act, both of whom get paid, then there are two middle spots normally only 5-10 minutes, these acts don't get paid so tend to be either new comics or acts trying new material, they are then followed by the headliner who obviously gets paid. The good thing about these spots is because they are in the middle of the show you should have an audience, unlike if you are an opening act for a big show, often the punters don't bother to see the first acts.

If you want to be a children's entertainer you can ask friends and family if they can set up a party for you to do, hopefully that will lead to more people wanting to to see your show.

So you now have a show, who else can book you?

Golf clubs and ladies nights.

If you are doing shows for adults, you can work your way up the comedy circuit but that can take some time to get to the paid gigs. There are lots of other venues that you might not have thought about for doing shows, Golf clubs regularly have entertainment. Masonic lodges, Rotary Clubs, and other clubs have entertainment, especially on "Ladies Nights" another source of regular work can be nursing homes and retirement villages, they have constant entertainment, they don't have big budgets but it's regular work.

If you want to work for children you can contact the Scouts and other such organisations but the majority of your work will probably be birthday parties. To a certain extent if you do a good show your birthday parties will roll on by word of mouth but If you are doing shows and people like you or if you are just talking about what you do, you are going to want to have something to hand out, you need a business card!

Business Cards

To me a good business card tells you everything you need to know in as few a words as possible. My favourite supplier for business cards is Moo. The great thing about Moo cards is that you can have up to 50 different photos on the backs of the cards. I have a few different pictures of different puppets that I use on the back of mine, this means that I can have picture of the figures I use in my adult shows that I hand out to people that I meet at comedy clubs and pictures of my dragon that I hand out to people I see at kids shows. On the front of my cards it just has my name, my phone number and my web site on it.

One of my Business Cards!

A picture paints a thousand words

The photos that you use say more about you than just what you look like. Make sure you have great photos, if your photos look amateurish then that's what people will think your show is going to be like.

Web Site

This is your window to the world! Make it fit your image and your "Brand" If someone has your business card then when they get to your website it should have the same "feel" about it, If a picture paints a thousand words then a video paints a million! Get a good video of your show and make a highlight, show reel no more than 3 minutes. This should show you off at you best, if it doesn't, don't surprised if the phone doesn't ring! After my entry in the Children's Entertainer of the Year competition in 2013, I put a highlights video on you tube, this was spotted by a woman who ran children's clubs in Cairo and she booked me for a weeks engagement.

HAVE YOU SEEN THIS DRAGON?

Friendly young Dragon.
Loves children. Very entertaining.
Answers to the name of Nigel.

0800 587 2931
www.SnotTheDragon.Com

This poster is given to every child that sees one of my shows

As well as my business cards and my web site I also have posters that every child from my show goes home with. This isn't just a poster, it has a story to it about when I lost my Dragon. The story ends up with me having all these posters that I don't know what to do with so I ask the children if anyone would like one, of course all the children want one so they all go home with my poster to put up on their walls!

Smile

Whenever you are dealing with the public, SMILE, it makes a great difference, be nice, be friendly you never know what a short conversation might lead to.

Booking the shows

To begin with, you will be able to keep track of your shows with just a diary but as time goes by you will need something a bit more robust. I use Giggio a booking system designed for performers. The great thing about Giggio is that you only have to enter the information once. When you have put the clients details and the venue and the show details in to the system it will generate a confirmation letter and an invoice, it will also but all the details into your diary and can be synced over all you devices, so when I am out and about and someone asks me if I can do a particular date not only can I see if I am free but if I am working it will have all the details of the job so I can see if I can fit them in, it has been one of my best investment in the last years, it also makes doing my tax returns so much easier.

One other advantage with Giggio is that you can export client's information for use with a mailing system such as MailChimp, that way you can send out newsletters to all your past clients with ease.

Where do I go From Here?

Well this is it, I have told you almost every thing I know about being a ventriloquist but this is where the fun starts, you are now on your way to being a ventriloquist so get out there, start performing and review your show as often as possible. You won't have perfect lip control at the start, it takes a lot of work but that should be your aim. People say that lip control doesn't matter, if the script is funny and you have good puppet manipulation that's all you need! Great lip control is what makes a great ventriloquist, If you don't want to work on lip control then get under the desk and call yourself a puppeteer.

There is a lot of free information on the internet, you can watch some great ventriloquists old and new on you tube. The International Ventriloquist Society is well worth checking out, you get lots of information from around the world.

Have fun and good luck in your new venture.

Colin Dymond

2014

Useful Information

Puppet Suppliers

The Puppet Hut

For a great range of puppets visit The Puppet Hut

The Puppet Hut is the biggest supplier of puppets in Europe. They are an official Axtell supplier and also stock Pavlov, Luna and many other great puppets. They also have the great new Vent masks by Peter Pullon

Jamie from The Puppet hut with a Luna Bison amongst others.

The Old Garage, Highstreet, Handcross, RH17 6BJ, 07725 418751

For everything Ventriloquial

Check out <u>MaherStudios.com</u> the home of The International Ventriloquist Society.

The International Ventriloquist Society

Being a member of the IVS gives you access to The IVS Spotlight a BiMonthly video magazine with interviews and top tips from ventriloquist from around the world. I am proud to be the UK corrispondant and hope to bring you all the news plus interviews with performers and puppet builders from the UK.

Colin Dymond

Colin has been a professional entertainer since 1996 and in that time has performed on every sized stage imaginable from theatres and cruise ships, to back room of a pub comedy nights or the local village hall.

He is President of the Cotswold Magical Society and Associate of The Inner Magic Circle with Silver Star!

His DVD "The Magic of Puppets" has sold worldwide and his first book "Making Magical Memories" is in The Magic Circle Library as well as on many a magician's shelves.

He has lectured across the United Kingdom and is always looking for the next adventure.

Lightning Source UK Ltd.
Milton Keynes UK
UKHW050943011118
331482UK00021B/287/P